Alkaline Ketogenic Smoothies

Easy and Delicious, Low-Carb, Low-Sugar Smoothies for a Healthy Lifestyle & Natural Weight Loss

By Elena Garcia
Copyright Elena Garcia © 2019

Sign up for new books, fresh tips, super healthy recipes, and our latest wellness releases:

www.YourWellnessBooks.com

Disclaimer

A physician has not written the information in this book. It is advisable that you visit a qualified dietician so that you can obtain a highly personalized treatment for your case, especially if you want to lose weight effectively. This book is for informational and educational purposes only and is not intended for medical purposes. Please consult your physician before making any drastic changes to your diet.

All information in this book has been carefully researched and checked for factual accuracy. However, the author and publishers make no warranty, expressed or implied, that the information contained herein is appropriate for every individual, situation or purpose, and assume no responsibility for errors or omission. The reader assumes the risk, and full responsibility for all actions and the author will not be held liable for any loss or damage, whether

Table of Contents

Introduction

Thank You for purchasing this book.
It means you are very serious about your health and wellbeing.

Whether your goal is to lose weight, enjoy more energy, or learn a few delicious healing smoothie recipes- you have come to the right place.

This recipe book is a practical guide designed for busy people who value their health and wellbeing.

To make it as doable and straightforward as possible:

1. We will start off with alkaline-keto shopping lists- so that you know what ingredients you need to focus on.
    You can even start taking action right away, as you are reading this book.

2. Then, I will guide you through straightforward explanations of the alkaline and keto diets, and how these two can be combined as well as the fantastic health and wellness benefits, you can experience by enriching your diet with nutrient-packed, low-carb, low-sugar alkaline keto smoothies.

3. Finally, I'll introduce you to my favorite alkaline-keto smoothie recipes. They are quick and easy to make. Just perfect for people who don't like cooking, or do not enjoy spending long hours in the kitchen. They are also great if you

are pressed for time- all you need is a blender and a few ingredients.

What I really like about alkaline-keto smoothies is that unlike traditional smoothies they don't use any high sugar fruit.

That makes them perfect for people who need to follow low-sugar, low-carb diets.

Another benefit is that they can be easily turned into delicious creamy soups (served raw or slightly cooked). You can easily customize your alkaline keto soups by adding in some protein of your choice to enjoy a satisfying, nutritious meal. The recipes contained in this book will show you how. Alkaline Keto Smoothies are much more than just smoothies!

Finally, the recipes, as well as "nutritional philosophies" contained in this book, are very flexible and open-minded. Anyone can benefit from them; they are not only for people who follow alkaline or keto diets. So, whether you are alkaline keto full-time, or merely part-time (you are looking for easy tips and recipes to improve your health), you have come to the right place!

I believe that just by creating a simple health habit of making one big alkaline keto smoothie a day, you have the power to transform your body and health.

The moment you decide to focus on abundance and enriching your diet with nutrient-packed, fresh foods (healthy foods that do not contain any nasty chemicals, sugars or crappy carbs) you will automatically crave all the good stuff.

So, without any further ado, let's do this. I am so excited for You!

Alkaline Keto Smoothies- Food Lists

Recommended Alkaline Keto Fruit

Both alkaline, as well as ketogenic diets, encourage you to stay away from sugar, including fruit that is high in sugar.

However, low-sugar fruits are allowed, and there are many ways to make them taste delicious (the recipes will show you how):

Alkaline Keto Approved Fruits:

- Limes
- Lemons
- Grapefruits
- Avocado (yes, it's a fruit)
- Tomato (yea, it's a fruit)
- Pomegranate

The following fruit is also allowed in small amounts:

- Blueberries
- Sour cherries
- Raspberries
- Strawberries
- Other berries
- Green apple (sparingly)

Recommended Alkaline Keto Greens

Greens are very good for you, and if used correctly, they will taste really nice in your smoothies. Don't worry if you have never made any green smoothies, or are not too sure how it will taste. The recipes contained in this book got you covered.

All leafy greens are super alkaline and also compatible with keto diets:

- Spinach
- Kale
- Microgreens
- Swiss Chard
- Arugula
- Endive
- Romaine Lettuce

+ other fresh leafy greens and greens as well as:

- Parsley
- Mint
- Chive
- Dill

I prefer fresh greens to green powders...but...whenever I go traveling, or I am really pressed for time, I use a delicious green powder blend called Organifi.

I also like to add it to my recipes as it makes my smoothies taste really nice while adding a ton of superfoods at the same time.

You can learn more about it and how I use it with my recipes on my website (treat it as an additional recommendation):

www.yourwellnessbooks.com/resources

Alkaline Keto Friendly Vegetables

All fresh veggies are considered alkaline, and most of them are also keto because they are low in carbs and low in sugar. The smoothie recipes from this book also call for good fats (more on the good fats later) to create alkaline keto balance.

So, these are the best alkaline – keto veggies to use in your smoothies:

- Red bell pepper
- Green bell pepper
- Yellow bell pepper
- Zucchini
- Broccoli
- Asparagus
- Colliflower
- Garlic
- Onion
- Cucumbers
- Radishes
- Artichokes

Alkaline Keto Spices & Herbs for Your Smoothies

The following herbs and spices will make your smoothies taste delicious.

They are also full of anti-inflammatory properties.

Again, since there are no sugars and no nasty carbs, the following herbs and spices are both alkaline and keto friendly.

- Cinnamon
- Himalaya Salt
- Curry
- Red Chili Powder
- Cumin
- Nutmeg
- Italian spices
- Oregano
- Rosemary
- Lavender
- Mint
- Chamomile
- Fennel
- Cilantro
- Moringa

The smoothie recipes from this book will give you guidelines as for how to use some of the herbs mentioned above to create specific, therapeutic smoothies, such as anti-insomnia smoothie, relaxation smoothie and more.

You will love it, I promise!

Alkaline Keto Sweeteners and Supplements (Optional)

Stevia (very helpful if you want to make a sweet smoothie without using sugar or sugar-containing foods or supplements)

- Green Powders
- Moringa Powder
- Maca Powder
- Ashwagandha Powder

Again, these are all optional. However, if you are interested in learning more, please visit our private website where I share more complimentary info with my readers. I have listed my favorite brands, green powders, and other health supplements to help you save your time:

www.YourWellnessBooks.com/resources

Alkaline Keto Fats

Plant-Based

(these are both alkaline and keto friendly)

- Olive oil (organic, cold-pressed)
- Avocado oil
- Hemp oil
- Flaxseed oil
- Coconut oil
- Sesame oil

(please note, there is no need to purchase all of them, one, or two is enough; my two favorites are coconut oil and olive oil)

Animal Based

(these are more keto than alkaline because the alkaline diet prefers plant-based products. However, they are OK to use on a balanced diet full of greens and veggies)

- Organic butter
- Fish oil

Alkaline Keto Nuts and Seeds

- Almonds (In moderation as they are richer in carbs)
- Cashews (in moderation as they are richer in carbs)
- Brazilian Nuts
- Macadamia Nuts
- Walnut
- Pine
- Pistachio
- Hazelnut

Alkaline Keto Friendly Milk & Other Liquids to Use in Smoothies

Plant-Based

(these are both alkaline and keto friendly)

- Almond milk
- Coconut milk
- Hazelnut milk
- Coconut water
- Herbal infusions
- Organic Apple Cider Vinegar

+ coffee and caffeine, in moderation.

Animal Based

(these are more keto than alkaline because the alkaline diet prefers plant-based products. However, they are OK to use on a balanced diet full of greens and veggies)

- Full-fat goat's milk (organic)
- Full-fat Greek yogurt (organic)
- Full-fat milk (organic)

You can skip these and use plant-based if you don't want to use dairy products.

If you have any questions about the food lists for alkaline keto smoothies, please email me at:

info@yourwellnessbooks.com

You can also sign up for our free newsletter at:

www.yourwellnessbooks.com/email-newsletter

and then reply to my first email and say hi.

Please note, the lists I have shared are basic food lists to make alkaline keto friendly smoothies because I want to keep it as simple as possible.

But they are not set in stone. I am always happy to answer your questions regarding the ingredients you want to use in your smoothies.

Now, let's move on to the next part!

Why Alkaline Ketogenic Smoothies? How Can They Help Us?

The problem is that most people eat way too many carbs and sugars. The temptations are everywhere, I know! To make it even worse, we eat processed carbs and sugars (pasta, candy, cakes, etc.). Most people find it hard to start their day without carbs and sugar.

Luckily, once you get into the alkaline ketogenic lifestyle, through adding more low carb, low sugar, high-fat smoothies into your diet, you will be able to experience a whole range of health and wellness benefits as well as possible prevention of many diseases.

Low carb, low sugar diets are proven to:

-manage your sugar levels, prevent diabetes

-normalize your hormones and auto-immune system

-improve your neurological health

-has even been used in clinical settings to prevent Alzheimer's, epilepsies, type 3 diabetes

Here are other benefits of aligning your dietary choices with an alkaline ketogenic-friendly way:

-you will experience reduced hunger and reduced cravings

-you will be burning fat and reducing carbs and so normalizing your insulin levels

-you will protect your heart while raising the good cholesterol

-you will enjoy the anti-age benefits, as keto foods promote longevity and vitality (while nobody ever promised us we will live forever, by making a decision to stay healthy, we make sure that the time we are here on earth, we feel good and are vibrant).

Your transformation starts right here, right now.

Alkaline Keto smoothies are one of the best and easiest tools to help you get started, even if you are busy.

Now, let's have a look at:

1. What the keto diet actually is.
2. What the alkaline diet is.
3. How these two can be successfully combined for optimal benefits while respecting your nutritional lifestyle choices and preferences.

The goal of this book is simple- I don't want to "push" any specific kind of a diet bandwagon or make you feel bad for eating a certain way.

Making people feel bad or fear-based marketing tactics never lead to any long-term transformation. Unfortunately, this is how most of the nutrition- health and fitness industry operates- fear-based marketing tactics and making people feel bad.

Instead, I want to inspire you and give you simple, healthy, and delicious tools (alkaline ketogenic smoothies) to help you get closer to your health, wellness, and fitness goals every day.

How about setting one simple goal, to begin with? Make 1 alkaline ketogenic smoothie a day? Take meaningful I and inspired action from a place of curiosity and empowerment, not fear.

Forget about perfection and focus on progress...

We are very, very close to help you get started. In fact, if you have already read my book *Alkaline Ketogenic Mix*, or *Alkaline Diet for Weight Loss and Wellness*, or *Alkaline Paleo Mix*, feel free to skip the following section and dive right into the recipes.

What really matters here is practice. But a little bit of inspiring information and learning more about our amazing bodies can also help.

So...

WHAT IS THE KETO DIET?

The simplest definition is:

The ketogenic diet is a diet low in carbs and high in healthy fats.

It encourages to massively reduce the carbohydrate intake and replace it with good, healthy fats (more on healthy vs. unhealthy fats later). This cutback in carbs puts your body into a metabolic state called ketosis.

When in ketosis, your body becomes super-efficient at burning fat for energy. A ketogenic diet can also help reduce blood sugar and insulin levels.

The fact is that we are designed to have periods where we "fast from carbs" and when our glucose levels are depleted.

Then, we start using our body very cleverly, using ketones for fuel. Ketones are the result of our body burning fat for food. The liver converts body fats and ingested fats into ketones.

Transition your diet into a more keto-friendly diet, it's straightforward. It means fewer sugars and carbs and more good fats while eating well!

Following this simple rule (even without going keto full-time) will help you transform your health. It will also help you lose weight naturally if you stay committed to it.

You will no longer be hooked on all those "crappy carbs" and with the new "keto energy" you will feel much more motivated to work out and be more active.

So, here's what the ketogenic diet consists of:

-75%- 80% fat (don't worry, it's all good fat and will not make you fat).

-5-15% healthy, clean protein

-5% good, unprocessed carbs (yea, you can still eat some carbs and the carbs we will be focusing on, will be healthy unprocessed no sugar carbs so no worries, there is no starvation involved here).

While it may seem like something hard to follow, especially when you still got that pasta meal on your mind, it will all become effortless after you get into the creamy, fatty, and actually guilt-free ketogenic friendly smoothie recipes!

WHAT IS THE ALKALINE DIET?

"Going green" is the way to describe an alkaline diet and lifestyle because the focus is on green vegetables in general, as they are the most alkaline food you can ingest.

The benefits of the alkaline diet are numerous. Let us name a few:

WEIGHT LOSS

An alkaline diet will assist you in losing weight. One way that it does this is obvious. The foods you will be eating are very healthy, rich in minerals and low calorie in general.

You will also be reducing the amount of acid in your body. The body stores fat to protect itself from an abundance of acid. It is a self-preservation method. This is part of the reason why people who exercise a lot and drink an excess of caffeine cannot seem to lose those extra pounds. Their bodies are clinging to that fat to minimize the effects of all of the acid in their systems. Caffeine is really acid-forming, and it's not the most sustainable source of energy. That is why we recommend you drink it in moderation, for your own occasional enjoyment rather than a source of energy you depend on.

Another benefit of an alkaline lifestyle regarding weight loss is that alkaline systems have more oxygen in their cells. Oxygen is a very essential part of eliminating fat cells from the body. The more oxygen in your system, the more efficient your metabolism will be.

ENERGY

Going green does not only give you energy for the apparent reason that you are eating many more healthy, energizing vitamins. You are negating the acid-induced lethargy that is brought on by an unhealthy acid-forming diet.

Not only do our bodies need an abundance of oxygen to lose weight, but we also need oxygen in our cells to energize us. The lack of oxygen in our cells causes fatigue. No, it is not just because you worked too late or partied to hard the night before. It is internal. If your cells are trying to function in a highly acidic environment, they will not be able to transfer oxygen efficiently; leading of course to exhaustion.

Cells in the body also make something that is called adenosine triphosphate (ATP). If your system is very acidic, it harms the ability of your cells to produce it. In the scientific world, it is known as the "energy currency of life." The ATP molecule contains the energy that we need to accomplish most things that we do (both internally and externally).

BODILY FUNCTIONS

Another benefit of the alkaline lifestyle is that your body will be able to function at an optimum level instead of being inhibited by acids:

- Your heartbeat is thrown off by acidic wastes in the body. The stomach suffers greatly from over-acidity.

- The liver's job is to get rid of acid toxins, but also to produce alkaline enzymes. By simply reducing your acid intake, you can internally boost your alkalinity thanks to your liver!

- Your pancreas thrives on alkalinity. Too much acid in your system throws off your pancreas. If you eat alkaline foods, your pancreas can regulate your blood sugars.

- Your kidneys also help to keep your body alkaline. When they are overwhelmed by an acidic diet, they cannot do their job

- The lymph fluids function most efficiently in an alkaline system. They remove acid waste. Acidic systems not only have a slower lymph flow causing acids to be stored; they can also cause acids to be reabsorbed through lymphatic ducts in your intestines that would typically be excreted.

MENTAL FOCUS

The alkalinity of the system is one of the best ways to focus and strengthen the mind. Just as the rest of the body is poorly affected by acid-forming foods and other toxins, so is your brain. And as we all know, it should be possible to control your emotions and decision making with your mind. Guess what? If your body is too acidic and is not alkaline, your mental clarity will be cloudy, your decision making could be off, as well as your emotional state.

DETOX

Another huge benefit of an alkaline lifestyle is detoxification. First, you are going to be cutting out processed foods that are continually adding toxins to your system.

Secondly, you are going to be eating foods that allow your body to detox and rid itself of the acids that have built up in your system all this time. When we detoxify our bodies, our emotions, bodily functions, and mental functions can operate at their optimum levels.

The number of benefits that come with living alkaline are numerous. As you help your body rebalance its optimal blood pH, you will find, as we did, that you have never felt better. We are still seeing improvement and reaping the rewards of this holistic approach to not only eating alkaline foods but living alkaline.

Alkaline vs. Acidic? Sounds like the title fight for a lightweight boxing match. In reality, it is a fight, a fight for the pH balance of your body. pH levels are basically the measure of how acidic a liquid is.

Our bodies function optimally when our blood is at about 7.35 - 7.45 pH.

pH levels range from 0 to 14. 0 is the highest level of acidity, but basically, everything 0-7 would be considered acidic. The 7-14 range is alkaline.

Before we dive into complicated pH discussions, here is one thing to understand:

-The alkaline <u>diet is not about changing or "raising" your pH</u>. This is where many alkaline guides go wrong. You see, our body is smart enough to **self-regulate** our pH for us, no matter what we eat.

Unfortunately, when you constantly bombard your body with acid-forming foods (for example processed foods, fast food, alcohol, sugar, crappy carbs, and even too much meat) you torture your body with incredible stress. Why? Well because it has to work harder to maintain that optimal pH…

Here's simple example...

Imagine you immerse yourself in a bath filled with ice. You say, but hey, my body can self-regulate its optimal temperature, right? And yes, it can. But it will eventually collapse, and you will get ill. The same happens with nutrition and our blood pH.

You can spend years indulging in toxic, processed, acid-forming foods that only deprive your body of its vital nutrients, saying: "But hey, my body will self-regulate its optimal blood pH."

And again, it will...but sooner or later it will give up and manifest a disease. It will accumulate fat as its natural defense function to protect your body from over-acidity. We don't wanna end up there, right?

So, to sum up- the alkaline diet is a natural, holistic system, a nutritional lifestyle that advocates the consumption of fresh, unprocessed foods that are rich in nutrients. These are called alkaline foods, and they help your body stimulate its optimal healing functions. Yes! A healthy body needs nutrients, and fresh fruits and vegetables are great for that.

The problem is that nowadays, most diets are filled with acid-forming foods that eventually make it hard for the body to regulate its optimal, healthy blood pH. Acidosis is very common in this day and age thanks to things we drink as well: coffee, alcohol, sugar, crappy carbs, and sodas all have an acidic effect on our bodies. Not to mention the chemicals many people take in through things like smoking and drugs (even prescription drugs have this effect).

There are many ways that you could become acidic. Eating acid-forming foods, stress, taking in too many toxins, and bodily processes all cause acidity in the body. Our internal systems try to balance themselves out and bring pH up with the help of alkaline minerals that we can ingest through our diet. If we do not take in a higher percentage of alkaline than acidic foods, we can become too acidic.

When you are acidic, it makes every process that your body does typically much more difficult or impossible for it to accomplish. We cannot absorb the beneficial nutrients we need from our food correctly. Our cells are not able to produce energy efficiently.

Our bodies are not able to fix damaged cells properly. We will not be able to detoxify properly. Fatigue and illness will drag you down. Sounds horrible; does it not? Here are some signs that you are overly acidic:

✓ Feeling tired all the time. You have no physical or mental drive at all.

✓ You always feel cold.

✓ You get sick easily.

✓ You are depressed or just feel "blah" all the time for no real reason

✓ You are easily overstimulated and stressed by noise, light, etc.

✓ You get headaches for no apparent reason

✓ You get watery eyes or inflamed eyelids.

✓ Your teeth are sensitive and may crack or chip

✓ Your gums are inflamed, and you are susceptible to canker sores

- ✓ You have recurring bouts with throat problems including tonsillitis

- ✓ Acidic stomach with acid indigestion and reflux is always an issue

- ✓ Your fingernails crack, split, and break

- ✓ You have super dry hair that sheds and is hay-like with split ends

- ✓ You have dry, ashy skin

- ✓ Your skin breaks out in acne or is irritated when you sweat

- ✓ You get leg cramps and spasms (this includes restless leg syndrome).

(Of course, remember that whenever you experience any health/medical conditions, you need to see your doctor first and get a checkup.)

Changing your diet to one that is full of alkaline foods is one of the easiest and best things you can do for your overall health. I was so ecstatic that I did! And the best thing is- we will be combining alkaline foods with keto friendly meals to make it easy, delicious and fun! Much simpler to follow for the long term.

But the way we see it is this- it's perfect! Plus, it's not a diet, it's a lifestyle.

What I really like about the alkaline diet is that you don't have to be 100% perfect. It's enough to make sure you add a ton of greens and veggies and make your diet rich in alkaline foods.

It's easy to do when you focus on serving your lunch or dinner with a big green salad or start drinking alkaline keto smoothies (I will show you how to go about it in the recipe section later).

When it comes to the alkaline diet, there is something called the 70/30 rule meaning that about 70% of your diet should be fresh, nutrient dense alkaline-forming foods and the remaining 30% can be acid- forming foods (however they still should be clean and organic, for example, grass-fed meat or organic eggs).

The common mistakes with the ketogenic diets:

The most common mistake that people make is that they do not include enough veggies with their keto animal-based foods. That can cause imbalance and acidity. Hence, I am such a big fan of keto and alkaline diets combined together. Green vegetables are a fantastic addition to your keto diet.

They will help you have more energy and also add more variety to your diet.

The real keto lifestyle is about variety, abundance, and energy. It's hard to be successful with a keto diet if a menu consists entirely of animal products.

The role of alkaline foods

It's essential to get a ton of greens and alkaline foods as these foods are rich in minerals and vitamins while at the same time don't contain sugar.

I have been promoting alkaline foods for years.

They oxygenate your body and help you have more energy and can be combined with other diets such as paleo or keto diet.

In its optimal design, alkaline diet advocates using good plant-based oils such as avocado and olive oil, and coconut oil and it also excludes wheat products and crappy carbs.

Foods that are rich in sugar are also excluded. The alkaline diet includes low sugar fruits (limes, lemons, grapefruits, etc.)

One of the main principles of the alkaline diet is adding a ton of green veggies into your diet.

The best way to be adding these alkaline foods is via low sugar and low carb alkaline keto smoothies! And you are already learning how to do that.

COMBINING ALKALINE WITH KETO

As surprising as it may sound, the ketogenic diet is actually pretty close to the alkaline diet.

The primary common rule is:

Eat real food, eat clean food. Relax. Reduce stress. Enjoy the nature...

And these are the alkaline-keto guidelines to help you create vibrant health and energy:

-add a lot of greens (one of the best ways is through the alkaline keto smoothies)

-add lots of healthy fats like omega 3 and saturated fats (again, alkaline keto smoothies will help you do that too)

-eat fresh, unrefined, natural foods

-get rid of processed carbs

-reduce fruit that is high in sugar (the recipes contained in this book only use low sugar fruit, and other fruit is used very sparingly, in small amounts, just to taste)

-eliminate gluten and sugar-containing foods and drinks

-get rid of refined oils

-consume moderate protein (alkaline diet focuses more on plant-based protein; however, some quality plant-based protein is also OK on this diet as long as you add in a ton of greens and veggies; similarly, while the keto diet is mostly known for recommending animal-based protein, plant-based protein from leafy greens, nuts and seeds is also keto-friendly)

Most smoothies use plant-based alkaline-keto protein. It would be pretty unusual to make a smoothie with bacon anyway. But, some vegetable smoothies can be turned into soups, and you can enrich them with some animal-based protein too. Believe it or not, my hubby loves putting bacon into his smoothie-veggie-soups.

The alkaline keto diet can be created in different versions.

Personally, I really enjoy plant-based foods and consume animal products in moderation (fish, eggs, Greek Yoghurt and some goat cheese here and there, are my favorites).

Whenever I go on a detox or a cleanse, I focus entirely on plant-based foods to give my digestive system a rest.

To learn more about the cleanses I do (which is a topic for another book), I highly recommend you visit:

www.YourWellnessBooks.com/resources

So, as you can see, the alkaline and keto diets are very similar and can easily be combined while respecting your personal preferences.

Your Wellness Books Email Newsletter

Before we dive into the recipes, we would like to offer you free access to our VIP Wellness Newsletter

www.yourwellnessbooks.com/email-newsletter

Here's what you will be receiving:
-healthy, clean food recipes and tips delivered to your email
-motivation and inspiration to help you stay on track
-discounts and giveaways
-notifications about our new books (at massively reduced prices)
-healthy eating resources to help you on your journey

No Fluff, no spam. Only excellent and easy to follow info!

Sign up link (copy this link to your phone, tablet, or PC):

Problems with signing up? Email us at:
info@yourwellnessbooks.com

www.yourwellnessbooks.com/email-newsletter

About the Recipes-Measurements Used in the Recipes

The cup measurement I use is the American Cup measurement.

I also use it for dry ingredients. If you are new to it, let me help you:

If you don't have American Cup measures, just use a metric or imperial liquid measuring jug and fill your jug with your ingredient to the corresponding level. Here's how to go about it:

1 American Cup= 250ml= 8 Fl.oz.

For example:

If a recipe calls for 1 cup of almonds, simply place your almonds into your measuring jug until it reaches the 250 ml/8oz marks.

I hope you found it helpful. I know that different countries use different measurements, and I wanted to make things simple for you. I have also noticed that very often those who are used to American Cup measurements complain about metric measurements and vice versa. However, if you apply what I have just explained, you will find it easy to use both.

Alkaline Keto Smoothie Recipes

These are great for all kinds of occasions and are just perfect if you don't have the time to cook. A nutritious vegetable smoothie with good fats in it will help you stay full for hours, and it is a terrific meal replacement. At the same time, many smoothies can be transformed into delicious, healing soups. With herbs, spices, and Himalaya salt, they will taste amazing. You can also add in some boiled eggs, fish, or some meat leftovers. It's effortless to create a healthy "meal" while on this lifestyle.

Alkaline keto soups can also be served as a side dish, and they always get people's attention.

Alkaline Keto Nourishing Smoothies You Will Love!

Green Dream Weight Loss Smoothie

This green vegetable smoothie blends the best of the alkaline and keto worlds. It's my number one recommendation if your goal is weight loss. It may take some time to get used to green vegetable smoothies. Especially if you are more accustomed to drinking "sweety-carby-fruity" smoothies (not that good for you, unfortunately).

But trust me, after a few green smoothies, and fantastic energy they provide, you will be wondering how you could ever live without them.

Himalaya salt really makes it taste delicious. Now, I like to keep my recipes as simple as possible, without too many ingredients.

But to let you know the variations of this recipe- you could also add in some cilantro, curry and chili pepper if you like spicy smoothies.

If you go for this variation, you may also heat up the smoothie and serve it as a beautiful, warm soup (and add some coconut or other full-fat cream on top). Enjoy!

Servings: 2

Ingredients:

- 1 cup coconut or almond milk (unsweetened)
- 1 cup water (filtered, preferably alkaline)
- 1 small avocado, peeled and pitted
- A handful of spinach
- 1 tablespoon coconut oil or flaxseed oil
- Pinch of Himalaya salt to taste

Instructions:

1. Place all the ingredients in a blender.
2. Blend well.
3. Serve and enjoy!

Seducing Bullet Proof Creamy Smoothie

This smoothie is called "seducing" for a reason.

It is perfect early in the morning to help you concentrate at work. It combines the antioxidant properties of blueberries with good fats and a bit of coffee.

While you don't want to end up in a position where you depend on caffeine, using it in small amounts to optimize your performance while nourishing your mind and body with a ton of alkaline nutrients will be very helpful! I love this smoothie for my long writing sessions.

Servings: 1-2

Ingredients:

- 1 strong expresso (use organic, quality coffee)
- 1 cup thick coconut milk
- A handful of organic blueberries
- 1 tablespoon chia seeds or chia seed powder
- Half teaspoon maca powder
- Half teaspoon cinnamon powder
- 2 tablespoons coconut oil

Instructions:

1. Blend all the ingredients except cinnamon powder.
2. Pour your smoothie into a smoothie glass and serve with ice cubes if needed.
3. Sprinkle some cinnamon powder on top.
4. Enjoy!

Keto Indulgent Fat Vitamin A Smoothie

This smoothie is a fantastic source of vitamin A to take care of your skin, eyes, and support a healthy immune system too.

Himalaya salt helps you add more alkaline minerals like Magnesium to your diet.

This smoothie can also be served as a thick, raw soup and you can add in some protein, for example, smoked salmon, or hard-boiled eggs.

Servings: 2

Ingredients:

- 1 cup Greek Yoghurt (full fat)
- 2 tablespoons organic butter
- 1 cup fresh parsley leaves, washed
- Half teaspoon Himalaya salt
- 2 tablespoon fresh cilantro leaves
- Black pepper (optional)

Instructions:

1. Place all the ingredients in a blender.
2. Process until smooth.
3. Serve and enjoy!
4. If needed, season with some black pepper.

***The following recipe will show you how to make a very similar smoothie in an entirely plant-based version.

Keto Indulgent Fat Vitamin A Smoothie – Plant-Based Version

This recipe is just perfect if you are looking for similar benefits that the last smoothie recipe offered, but you prefer fully plant-based recipe, or you just love coconut!

Servings: 2

Ingredients:

- 1 cup thick coconut milk (full fat)
- 2 tablespoons coconut oil
- Half avocado, peeled and sliced
- Half lemon, peeled and sliced
- 1 cup fresh parsley leaves, washed
- Half teaspoon Himalaya salt
- 2 tablespoons fresh cilantro leaves
- Black pepper (optional)

Instructions:

1. Place all the ingredients in a blender.
2. Process until smooth.
3. Serve and enjoy!
4. If needed season with some black pepper.

Creamy Relaxation Smoothie

This smoothie uses healing herbal infusions such as chamomile and rooibos.

Chamomile is famous for its sleep and calm-inducing properties, while rooibos is full of alkaline ingredients. It's also naturally sweet, and so is this smoothie.

Servings: 2-3

Ingredients:

- 1 cup rooibos tea (cooled down, use 1 teabag per cup)
- 1 cup chamomile tea (cooled down, use 1 teabag per cup)
- 1 small avocado, peeled and pitted
- 1 small lime, peeled and sliced
- Half cup thick coconut milk
- 2 tablespoons coconut oil
- 1 teaspoon cinnamon powder
- A handful of cashews
- Stevia to sweeten if needed

Instructions:

1. Place all the ingredients in a blender.
2. Process until smooth.
3. Enjoy now or place in a fridge for later.

Easy Spicy Veggie Smoothie

This smoothie will help you enrich your diet with healthy, alkalizing vegetables. I like to make this smoothie in the evening and use one serving as a quick detox soup (yea, you can heat it up a bit) and then I keep the second serving as a quick morning smoothie.

Servings: 2

Ingredients:

- 1 green bell pepper
- 1 small avocado, peeled and pitted
- 1 small garlic clove, peeled
- Pinch of black pepper and chili
- 1 cup water (filtered, or alkaline water)
- 1 tablespoon extra-virgin olive oil
- Himalaya salt to taste

Instructions:

1. Place all the ingredients in a blender.
2. Process until smooth, serve, and enjoy!

Simple Anti-Inflammatory Alkaline Keto Mix

This smoothie is perfect if your goal is to have more energy and reduce inflammation.

It focuses on two highly anti-inflammatory ingredients- turmeric and ginger. Fresh almond milk is very alkalizing and rich in natural protein. Good fats will help you stay full and focused for hours. Maca powder is optional here. Personally, I love it!

When peeling turmeric, I recommend you use gloves. Otherwise, you may end up with orange nails and hands for a couple of days.

Servings: 1-2

- 1 cup fresh almond milk, unsweetened
- Half cup water, filtered, preferably alkaline water
- 2-inch ginger, peeled
- 2-inch turmeric, peeled
- Half avocado, peeled and pitted
- 1 tablespoon coconut oil
- Stevia to sweeten (optional)

Instructions:

1. Blend and enjoy.
2. Add some stevia to sweeten if needed.
3. This drink is great first thing in the morning. But you can also sip on it during the day to enjoy more energy.

Coconut Almond Protein Balancer

This delicious smoothie uses stevia (both alkaline and keto friendly natural sweetener) so that you can enjoy an excellent, creamy sweet taste.

It also uses maca powder, which is a hormone re-balancer for women.

Enjoy!

Ingredients:

- 1 cup coconut milk, unsweetened
- A handful of almonds (raw, unsweetened and soaked in filtered, alkaline water for a few hours)
- 1 tablespoon coconut oil
- A bit of stevia to sweeten
- Half teaspoon fresh maca powder

+ a few lime slices and ice cubes to serve if needed

Instructions:

1. Place all the ingredients in a blender.
2. Process until smooth.
3. Serve and enjoy!
4. This smoothie also tastes delicious when chilled or half frozen.

Cucumber Dream Creamy Cheesy Smoothie

This is one of my favorite "on the go" smoothie recipes as it doesn't require that many ingredients.

It can also be transformed into a delicious raw soup.

I have created a fully plant-based version of this recipe which you can check out on the next page.

Servings: 2-3

Ingredients:

- 2 big cucumbers, peeled and roughly sliced
- 1 cup full-fat Greek Yoghurt
- 4 tablespoons grated goat cheese
- Pinch of Himalaya salt to taste
- Pinch of black pepper to taste
- 6 radishes, sliced
- 2 tablespoons chive, chopped

Instructions:

1. Place the cucumbers, and Greek Yoghurt in a blender.
2. Add the Himalaya salt and black pepper.
3. Blend well and pour into a smoothie glass or a small soup bowl.
4. Add in the radishes and chive.
5. Mix well and add more Himalaya salt and black pepper if needed.
6. Sprinkle the cheese and enjoy!

Cucumber Dream Creamy Plant Based Alkaline Smoothie

This is a plant-based version of the previous recipe. It also tastes delicious, and I highly recommend it for days where your goal is detoxification to have more energy.

Servings: 2-3

Ingredients:

- 2 big cucumbers, peeled and roughly sliced
- 1 big avocado
- 1 cup of coconut milk
- 1 small lemon, peeled and sliced
- 4 tablespoons cashews, chopped or powdered
- Pinch of Himalaya salt to taste
- Pinch of black pepper to taste
- 6 radishes, sliced
- 2 tablespoons chive, chopped

Instructions:

1. Place the cucumbers, coconut milk, avocado and lemon in a blender.
2. Add the Himalaya salt and black pepper.
3. Blend well and pour into a smoothie glass or a small soup bowl.
4. Add in the radishes and chive.
5. Mix well and add more Himalaya salt and black pepper if needed.
6. Sprinkle the cashews and enjoy!

Refreshing Radish Liver Lover Smoothie

Radish is a fantastic alkaline keto veggie that is very often overlooked. I always say there is no need to look for expensive and over-priced superfoods. Why not focus on what is already freely available? Radishes are very alkalizing and good for your liver and immune system. They are also very refreshing!

Servings: 1-2

Ingredients:

- Half cup radish, washed
- 1 small avocado, peeled and pitted
- A handful of fresh arugula leaves
- 1 cup full-fat coconut milk (no added sugar)
- Half cup of water
- Pinch of Himalaya salt to taste
- Pinch of black pepper to taste
- Optional: red chili pepper

Instructions:

1. Blend all the ingredients.
2. Serve in a smoothie glass or in a soup bowl- this smoothie can also be turned into a delicious soup.

If you serve this smoothie as a soup, feel free to add in some protein. It can be plant-based protein, for example, some nuts and seeds, or hard-boiled eggs. My husband loves to add in some smoked salmon or bacon.

Experiment with different options and let us know your experience by posting a review on Amazon.

Cilantro Oriental Alkaline Keto Smoothie

Cilantro is a miraculous alkaline herb with potent antioxidant properties. While making a curry can be very time-consuming, why not enjoy cilantro in a simple smoothie that you can make in less than 5 minutes).

Servings: 2-3

Ingredients:

- 2 cups coconut or almond milk
- 2 tablespoons coconut oil
- A handful of fresh cilantro leaves
- 1 small red bell pepper, sliced and seeded
- 1 teaspoon curry powder
- Pinch of Himalaya salt to taste
- Pinch of black pepper powder to taste

Instructions:

1. Combine all the ingredients in a blender.
2. Process until smooth.
3. Taste to check if you need to add more salt or spices.
4. Pour into a smoothie glass or a small soup bowl and enjoy!

Vitamin C Alkaline Keto Power

This delicious smoothie is jam-packed with vitamin C coming from alkaline and keto friendly fruits like limes and lemons. Now, I understand that looking at the ingredients of this recipe, you may be feeling a bit "turned off." Yes, alkaline keto smoothies are very different to usual "sweet fruity smoothies."

But, give it a try. It tastes great! Very similar to natural, Greek yogurt. You can also use this smoothie recipe to season your salads. Most salad seasonings are full of crappy carbs, sugars and a ton of chemicals, while this smoothie is 100% natural! Another suggestion is - you could use this smoothie recipe to make a smoothie bowl by adding in some nuts and seeds. Once you have tried this smoothie, you will get my point for sure!

Servings: 2

Ingredients:

- 1 big avocado, peeled, pitted and sliced
- Half lemon, peeled and sliced
- 1 cup of coconut milk
- 1 teaspoon coconut oil
- Pinch of Himalaya salt
- Pinch of black pepper
- A few slices of lime to garnish

Instructions:

1. Place all the ingredients in a blender.
2. Process until smooth.
3. Serve in a smoothie glass and garnish with a few lime slices.
4. Drink to your health and enjoy!

Hormone Rebalancer Natural Energy Smoothie

This smoothie recipe is a fantastic option if you don't like green smoothies, but you still want to experience all the health benefits of alkaline keto smoothies.

This recipe uses stevia which is a natural sweetener, very often used both on keto and alkaline diets.

Although, let me remind you that once your taste buds have adapted, you will be able to do without any sweeteners easily.

Still, if you need one- go for stevia.

Servings: 1-2

Ingredients:

- 1 big grapefruit, peeled and halved
- 1 cup water (filtered, preferably alkaline)
- 1 inch of ginger, peeled
- 1 tablespoon coconut oil
- Half teaspoon maca powder
- Stevia to sweeten, if desired

Instructions:

1. Blend all the ingredients in a blender.
2. Serve and enjoy!

Green Mineral Comfort Smoothie Soup

This recipe can be used both as a smoothie as well as a soup.

Whenever I am pressed for time, I make it for dinner, to enjoy something warm and keep the raw leftovers to have a healthy green smoothie in the morning.

Servings: 1-2

Ingredients:

- 1 big cucumber, peeled
- 1 small avocado, peeled and pitted
- A handful of parsley
- A handful of cilantro
- 1 cup of thick coconut milk
- A handful of raw cashews
- 1 tablespoon of olive oil
- Himalaya salt to taste
- 1 chili flake

Instructions:

1. Blend all the ingredients in a blender.
2. Serve raw as a smoothie, or heat it up (using low heat) and serve as a gentle, detox, comforting soup.
3. Enjoy!

White Creamy Buttery "Smoothie" Soup

This super easy recipe needs only five ingredients (seasonings included).

It's perfect if you crave something creamy. My secret addiction (for many years) was bread with butter. And, for years I was convinced it was the bread I wanted. However, after transitioning my diet to a more keto friendly lifestyle, I realized I no longer crave bread. All I need is a little butter!

This recipe also uses healing alkaline veggies like cauliflower, and, at the same time, adds in some garlic to help you strengthen your immune system.

Servings: 1-2

Ingredients:

- 1 cup cauliflower, slightly cooked or steamed, cut into smaller pieces
- 4 tablespoons organic butter (you can also use coconut oil instead)
- 1 cup water (filtered, preferably alkaline)
- 2 garlic cloves, peeled and minced
- Himalaya salt

Instructions:

1. In a small pot, combine the butter and garlic.
2. Fry the garlic on low heat.
3. Cover.
4. In the meantime, using a blender, combine the cooked cauliflower, 2 pinches of Himalaya salt and water.
5. Now add the mixture to the pot with butter and garlic.
6. Simmer on low heat until the soup is warm and creamy.
7. If needed, add more Himalaya salt to taste (as well as other spices if desired). Enjoy!

Creamy Cauliflower Smoothie

I have developed this recipe by accident. As I was doing research about health and wellness benefits of cauliflower (super rich in nutrients, low in calories, helps in weight loss etc.) I asked myself: how can I add more of that miraculous super veggie into my diet? Prior to that I had never been a big cauliflower fan. Well...not until I developed this delicious alkaline keto friendly recipe...

Servings: 2-3

Ingredients:

- 1 cup cauliflower florets, steamed or lightly cooked
- 2 tablespoons organic butter
- 1 cup full-fat kefir or Greek Yoghurt (organic, unflavored)
- 10 radishes, sliced
- Half red onion, minced
- 1 garlic clove, peeled
- Black pepper and chili powder to taste
- Himalaya salt to taste

Instructions:

1. Place all the ingredients, except the radishes and onion into a blender.
2. Process until smooth.
3. Serve in a smoothie glass or a small soup bowls and add in the radishes and onion.
4. If needed, add more salt and spices.
5. Enjoy!

Creamy Cauliflower Green Alkaline Smoothie

This recipe is a slight modification of the previous one, in an entirely plant-based alkaline version that also incorporates some greens. This recipe is perfect for detox. One of my favorite detoxes is Yuri Elkaim's cleanse. You can learn more about it on my website:

www.YourWellnessBooks.com/resources

Now, let's dive into the recipe

Servings: 2-3

Ingredients:

- 1 cup cauliflower florets, steamed or lightly cooked
- 2 tablespoons olive oil or avocado oil
- 1 cup coconut or hazelnut or almond milk
- 1 medium-sized avocado, peeled and sliced
- Half cup water, filtered, preferably alkaline
- 1 cup fresh arugula leaves, washed
- 10 radishes, sliced
- Half red onion, minced
- 1 garlic clove, peeled
- Black pepper and chili powder to taste
- Himalaya salt to taste

Instructions:

1. Place all the ingredients, except the radishes and onion into a blender.
2. Process until smooth.
3. Serve in a smoothie glass or a small soup bowls and add in the radishes and onion.
4. If needed, add more salt and spices.
5. Enjoy!

Beautiful Skin Healthy Glow Smoothie

Red bell peppers are naturally sweet and very good for you. When using turmeric, I recommend you use gloves, unless you want to walk around with orange nails and hands for the next couple of days.

Servings: 2

Ingredients:

- 2 red bell peppers, sliced, seeds removed
- 1-inch turmeric, peeled
- 1-inch ginger, peeled
- 1 cup coconut cream or full-fat Greek Yoghurt
- 2 tablespoons avocado oil or flax seed oil
- 1 cup water, filtered, preferably alkaline
- 1 teaspoon cinnamon powder
- 2 tablespoons hemp seed or chia seed powder
- Stevia, to sweeten (optional)

Instructions:

1. Combine all the ingredients in a blender.
2. Process well until smooth.
3. If needed, sweeten with stevia.
4. Serve and enjoy!

Spicy Creamy Rebalancer

This smoothie is full of vitamins A and E to help you have beautiful skin and healthy eyesight. Cinnamon makes it naturally sweet, and the color is just amazing! Ashwagandha is a miraculous herb and a natural balancer. Personally, I love this smoothie in the afternoon. It gives me a nice energy boost, but at the same time helps me relax so that I can regulate my sleep cycle. If you want to learn more about Ashwagandha I recommend you read my book:

ASHWAGANDHA: The Miraculous Herb!: Holistic Solutions & Proven Healing Recipes for Health, Beauty, Weight Loss & Hormone Balance

Now, back to the recipe...

Servings: 2

Ingredients:

- 2 medium-sized carrots, peeled
- 1-inch turmeric
- 1 teaspoon cinnamon powder
- Half teaspoon Ashwagandha powder
- 2 cups full fat coconut milk, or full-fat goat milk
- 2 tablespoons coconut oil or avocado oil
- 1 tablespoon chia seeds

Instructions:

1. Place all the ingredients in a blender.
2. Process well until smooth.
3. Serve and enjoy!

Italian Herbs Antioxidant Smoothie

Not only is this smoothie refreshing and full of antioxidant properties.

It can also be turned into a delicious soup that can be served both in an entirely plant-based version, or "cheesy vegetarian" version.

The second option is great if you are craving pizza...and much healthier for you, especially if you want to lose weight naturally and relatively fast.

Servings: 2

Ingredients:

- 4 big organic tomatoes
- 1 tablespoon Italian spices
- Pinch of Himalaya salt
- 1 garlic clove, peeled
- 1 cup water, filtered, preferably alkaline
- 2 tablespoons olive oil
- 2 tablespoons almonds, soaked in filtered water for at least 3-4 hours
- Half cup mixed olives (green and black), pitted

Instructions:

1. Place all the ingredients in a blender.
2. Process well until smooth.
3. Pour into a smoothie glass and enjoy!
4. Or...turn into a naughty cheese soup (recipe on the next page!)

Italian Herbs Antioxidant Cheesy Soup

Now, it's time to turn the smoothie from the previous recipe into a delicious soup...

Servings: 2

Ingredients:

- Italian Herbs Antioxidant Smoothie from the last recipe
- 1 big onion, minced
- 4 big slices of organic goat cheese
- 1 tablespoon coconut oil or organic butter
- 1 tablespoon Italian spices

Instructions:

1. Using a medium-sized skillet on medium heat, start stir-frying onions in coconut oil or butter.
2. When slightly brown, add the cheese and spices and keep stir-frying.
3. As soon as the cheese starts melting, lower the heat to low heat.
4. Now pour in the Italian Herbs Antioxidant Smoothie.
5. Stir-fry on low heat for a few minutes so that the "smoothie soup" gets slightly warm and absorbs the flavor of the cheese and spices.
6. Turn off the heat and enjoy!

Green Fat Burner Smoothie

This recipe combines the best fat-burning ingredients ever, helps you concentrate for long hours while feeling lighter.

It's also great if you suffer from water retention. Personally, I love drinking this smoothie in the summer.

Servings: 2

Ingredients:

- 1 green tea teabag (or 1 teaspoon green tea powder)
- 1 horsetail infusion tea bag (or 1 teaspoon horsetail infusion powder)
- 1 cup of water
- 1 big avocado
- 1 big grapefruit
- Half cup of coconut milk
- 1 teaspoon cinnamon powder
- Stevia to sweeten

Instructions:

1. Boil 1 cup of water.
2. Add in the green tea and horsetail infusion.
3. Cover.
4. In the meantime, process the remaining ingredients in a blender.
5. Add in the cooled herbal infusion and process again.
6. If needed sweeten with stevia.
7. Serve chilled and enjoy!

Anti-Flu Mediterranean Keto "Smoothie Soup"

This is another, super easy recipe that you can enjoy both as a quick, raw smoothie, or a beautiful, healing soup (raw or slightly cooked).

It's full of anti-inflammatory properties, and it also helps fight colds and flu.

Servings: 1-2

Ingredients:

- 4 medium-sized tomatoes, peeled
- 1 big garlic clove, peeled
- 4 small celery sticks
- 2 tablespoons olive oil
- A handful of black olives
- Half cup water, preferably alkaline (or filtered water)
- Himalaya salt to taste
- 1 teaspoon oregano
- A few fresh basil leaves
- 1 hard-boiled egg (optional)

Instructions:

1. Combine all the ingredients in a blender.
2. Process well until smooth. Add more water if needed.
3. Serve in a smoothie or soup bowl and add in a hard-boiled egg.
4. Serve and enjoy!

Massive Green Power Plants Smoothie

If you don't like spinach or kale, I highly recommend you try arugula leaves. They taste delicious, both in salads and smoothies.

Servings: 3-4

Ingredients:

- 1 cup arugula leaves, washed
- 1 small avocado, peeled, pitted and sliced
- 2 cucumbers, peeled and sliced
- 4 tablespoons fresh lemon juice
- 2 tablespoons olive oil
- 2 cups hazelnut milk (unsweetened)
- Himalaya salt and black pepper to taste

Instructions:

1. Place all the ingredients in a blender.
2. Process well until smooth.
3. Serve and enjoy!

Irresistible Mediterranean Dream

This smoothie is perfect if you are pressed for time and are looking for a quick and healthy way to put a nice, nourishing meal-replacing smoothie together.

Servings: 2

Ingredients:

- 1 cup of mixed greens (I like arugula and kale)
- 2 tomatoes, sliced
- A few onion rings
- 6 big slices of goat cheese (preferably organic)
- A few slices of avocado
- Half cup of green olives
- 1 tablespoon lemon juice
- 1 cup water, filtered, preferably alkaline
- 2 tablespoons olive oil (organic)

Instructions:

1. Place all the ingredients in a blender.
2. Process well until smooth.
3. Serve and enjoy!

(yes, a little bit of goat's cheese in a smoothie really makes it taste delicious!)

Easy Creamy Plant Based Smoothie

Cashews are definitely one of my favorite alkaline keto ingredients for creamy, plant-based smoothies like this one.

Servings: 1-2

Ingredients:

- Half cup raw cashews, crushed
- 2 tablespoons of coconut oil
- 1 cup green bell pepper
- Himalaya salt and black pepper to taste
- 1 cup water, filtered, preferably alkaline

Instructions:

1. Place all the ingredients in a blender.
2. Process well until smooth.
3. Serve and enjoy!

Alkaline Keto Protein Smoothie

Hazelnuts not only make this smoothie taste amazing, but they also add in good fats and protein. Pomegranates are 100% alkaline keto approved as they are low in sugar and super high in alkaline minerals.

Servings: 2-3

Ingredients:

- Half cup hazelnuts, soaked in water
- 2 tablespoons coconut oil
- 2 cups of water
- 1 teaspoon cinnamon powder
- 1 teaspoon maca powder
- Half cup pomegranates

Instructions:

1. Place all the ingredients in a blender.
2. Process well until smooth.
3. Serve and enjoy!

Electrolytes Balance Weight Loss Smoothie

Grapefruit is a fantastic fruit that is both alkaline and keto friendly. It's because it is full of alkaline minerals like magnesium and potassium, while at the same time, it's a low sugar fruit. Exactly what we want on this diet and lifestyle!

It blends really well with coconut water. This smoothie is low in calories, high in fats and miraculous nutrients. It's perfect after a strenuous workout.

Servings: 1-2

Ingredients:

- 1 grapefruit, peeled
- 1 cup coconut water, unsweetened
- A handful of fresh mint leaves
- Pinch of Himalaya salt
- 2 tablespoons of coconut oil
- Stevia to sweeten if needed

Instructions:

1. Place all the ingredients in a blender.
2. Process well until smooth.
3. Serve and enjoy!

Easy Guacamole Smoothie

This smoothie can also be used as a dip to be served with some veggies.

It also makes a great meal replacement if you are pressed for time and are looking for an easy and nutritious meal.

Servings: 1-2

Ingredients:

- 2 tomatoes, sliced
- Half avocado, peeled and sliced
- A handful of arugula leaves
- 1 small garlic clove, peeled and minced
- 4 tablespoons lime juice
- Half cup water, filtered
- 2 tablespoons olive oil
- Himalaya salt and black pepper to taste

Instructions:

1. Place all the ingredients in a blender.
2. Process well until smooth.
3. Serve and enjoy!

Easy Balance Fennel Smoothie

Fennel is an intensely aromatic, naturally sweet (but alkaline keto approved) ingredient that tastes really delicious in smoothies.

Ginger is a fantastic addition to this smoothie- it's full of anti-inflammatory properties and also helps strengthen the immune system.

Enjoy!

Servings: 1-2

Ingredients:

- 1 fennel bulb cut into smaller pieces
- 1 cup thick coconut milk
- 1 tablespoon coconut oil
- Pinch of Himalaya salt
- 1 tablespoon grated ginger

Instructions:

1. Place all the ingredients in a blender.
2. Process well until smooth.
3. Serve and enjoy!

Sexy Spicy Turmeric Anti-Pain Smoothie

This smoothie is great if you need something to warm up or fight the cold or flu. It's full of antioxidant ingredients.

Servings: 1-2

Ingredients:

- Half teaspoon turmeric powder
- Pinch of black pepper
- 2 tablespoons coconut oil
- A pinch of chili powder
- Half teaspoon curry powder
- Himalaya salt to taste
- 1 cup almond or coconut milk
- 2 tablespoons coconut oil
- 1-inch ginger, peeled
- A few carrot slices

Instructions:

1. Place all the ingredients in a blender.
2. Process well until smooth.
3. Serve as raw or slightly cooked and enjoy!

Ginger and Turmeric Hormone Balancing Smoothie

This smoothie is yet another excellent recipe to help you fight off coughs and colds and will perform wonders for those looking to lose excess weight. It blends good fats with nutrition and alkalizing herbs.

Himalaya salt is very good for you and full of alkaline minerals. Black pepper helps in turmeric absorption, and so it's good to mix the two ingredients in one recipe.

Serves: 1

Ingredients:

- 2-inch ginger, peeled
- 2-inch turmeric, peeled
- 1 cup water, filtered, preferably alkaline
- 2 tablespoons coconut oil
- Half teaspoon of Ashwagandha powder
- 2 slices of lime
- Pinch of Himalaya salt and black pepper

Instructions:

1. Place all the ingredients in a blender.
2. Process until, smooth.
3. Serve and enjoy!

Easy Chili Tea Smoothie

This smoothie will help in cleansing your digestive tract while warming you up and giving you a substantial energy boost that will last for hours.

Serves: 2
Ingredients:

- 1 cup rooibos tea (use 2 teabags per 1 cup of water), warm but not hot
- 1 red chili flake or a pinch of red chili powder
- Half avocado, peeled and pitted
- A handful of fresh cilantro
- 2 tablespoons coconut oil or ghee

Instructions:

1. Place all the ingredients in a blender.
2. Process well until smooth.
3. Serve and enjoy!

Cumin No More Cramps Smoothie

This smoothie is an excellent recipe for women looking to obtain relief from period cramps. Adding in some good fats enhances the therapeutic properties of this alkaline keto style smoothie. It's also full of antioxidant properties, thanks to ginger and greens.

Serves: 1-2
Ingredients:

- 1 cup thick coconut milk
- 1-inch ginger, peeled
- Half teaspoon cumin seed powder
- Half avocado, peeled and pitted
- Pinch of Himalaya salt to taste
- 2 tablespoons coconut oil or avocado oil

Instructions:

1. Place all the ingredients in a blender.
2. Process well until smooth.
3. Serve and enjoy!

Spicy Chai Tea Smoothie

This smoothie uses chai tea and is super tasty and creamy. It's great to prevent colds too. It's one of my favorite comfort, alkaline keto smoothies. Black chai tea contains theine, and it's great to help you focus. I love this creamy oriental smoothie for my long writing sessions.

Serves: 1-2
Ingredients:
- 1 cup chai tea (use 1 Indian chai tea bag per 1 cup of water), cooled down
- 1-inch turmeric, peeled
- Half cup pomegranates
- Half cup coconut cream
- 1 tablespoon coconut oil

Instructions:

1. Place all the ingredients in a blender.
2. Process well until smooth.
3. Serve and enjoy!

***In the absence of chai tea, make use of black tea leaves mixed with cinnamon, cloves, and cardamom.

Ashwagandha Alkaline Keto Smoothie

This smoothie is an excellent herbal recipe for those looking to increase their immunity and balance. Personally, I like this tea at night-time as it helps me sleep like a baby. Sour cherries are a natural source of melatonin to add to the therapeutic properties of this smoothie.

Serves: 1-2
Ingredients:
- Half teaspoon dried Ashwagandha
- Half cup sour cherries pitted
- 1 cup coconut or almond milk
- Half avocado pitted and peeled
- Stevia to sweeten, if needed

Instructions:

1. Place all the ingredients in a blender.
2. Process well until smooth.
3. Serve and enjoy!

Sleep Well Aroma Smoothie

This recipe will help you unwind after a busy day to sleep like a baby, and wake up feeling energized. The cinnamon powder makes this smoothie naturally sweet, without compromising its no sugar alkaline keto friendly guidelines.

Serves: 2

Ingredients:

- 1 cup chamomile tea (use 1 tea bag per 1 cup of water), chilled
- Half avocado, peeled and pitted
- A few slices of fresh fennel bulb
- 1 tablespoon of coconut oil
- 1 teaspoon cinnamon powder
- Stevia to sweeten if needed

Instructions:

1. Place all the ingredients in a blender.
2. Process well until smooth.
3. Serve and enjoy!

Easy Mediterranean Relaxation Smoothie

It's time for another relaxing alkaline keto smoothie! Aside from its relaxing properties, rosemary and fennel are both miraculous herbs and will help you boost your immune system and fight off colds and flu. Fennel is also great for weight loss as well as stimulating your lymphatic system. It's amazing how many health benefits one simple smoothie can have.

Serves: 2

Ingredients:

- 1 cup boiling water
- 1 teaspoon rosemary herb
- 1 teaspoon fennel seeds
- 1 tablespoon coconut oil
- Half cup almond milk
- Half avocado
- Stevia to sweeten if needed
- 2 slices of lime to serve

Instructions:

1. In a small teacup or teapot, combine the boiling water with rosemary and fennel seeds.
2. Cover and set aside to cool down.
3. In the meantime, blend the avocado with almond milk.
4. Add in the cooled herbal infusion and blend again.
5. Serve with some fresh lime slices and, if needed, season with stevia.
6. Enjoy!

Lime Refresher Ice Smoothie

This smoothie combines the best of alkaline keto fruits and herbs to help you enjoy energy and vitality. It's super refreshing as well!

Servings: 2

Ingredients

- 2 grapefruits, peeled and sliced
- 2 limes, peeled and sliced
- 1 tablespoon fresh oregano
- 1 cup almond milk
- 1 tablespoon avocado oil

Instructions:

1. Place all the ingredients in a blender.
2. Process well until smooth.
3. Serve and enjoy!

Cucumber Kale Alkaline Keto Smoothies

Avocado oil offers good fat to help you absorb the minerals and vitamins from this smoothie. Celery stalks are full of vitamins and minerals, including vitamin K, vitamin A, potassium, and folate. Personally, I love using hot habanero sauce in my veggie smoothies. Who said that all smoothies must be sweet?

Servings: 3-4
Ingredients:
- 1 lemon, peeled
- 3 celery stalks, chopped
- A couple dashes of hot habanero sauce
- a handful of kale, chopped
- 2 big cucumbers, peeled and chopped
- 2 tablespoons of avocado oil
- Himalaya salt to taste
- 1 cup of water (filtered or alkaline)
- 1 cup of organic tomato juice

Instructions:
1. Place all the ingredients in a blender.
2. Process well until smooth.
3. Serve and enjoy!

Sexy Flavored Spinach Smoothie

While pure spinach smoothie can be a bit boring, this recipe is a bit different.

Add in some fresh ginger and mix it with coconut milk and oil, and you will fall in love with spinach smoothie!

Serves: 2

Ingredients:

- Half cup of baby spinach
- 2-inch ginger, peeled
- 2 tablespoons coconut oil
- 1 cup of coconut milk

Instructions:

1. Place all the ingredients in a blender.
2. Process well until smooth.
3. Serve and enjoy!

Red Bell Pepper Antioxidant Smoothie

Red bell pepper, ginger, and healing greens is an excellent combination.
It makes the smoothie taste nice even if you are new to green drinks.

Servings: 2
Ingredients:
- 1 big red bell pepper, chopped
- A handful of mixed leafy greens of your choice
- 2 inch of ginger, peeled
- 2 tablespoons avocado or olive oil
- 1 cup hazelnut milk
- Himalaya salt to taste

Instructions:

1. Place all the ingredients in a blender.
2. Process well until smooth.
3. Serve and enjoy!

Simple Lemon Smoothie

This smoothie helps maintain a healthy digestive system. It's also great for detox.

Servings: 2
Ingredients:

- A handful of fresh mint leaves
- 1 lemon, peeled and sliced
- 1 cup water, filtered, preferably alkaline
- Pinch of Himalaya salt
- 2 tablespoons avocado oil

Instructions:

1. Place all the ingredients in a blender.
2. Process well until smooth.
3. Serve and enjoy!

Optimal Hydration Mineral Green Smoothie

This is a super hydrating smoothie. It's jam-packed with energy restoring alkaline minerals and healthy fats.

Servings: 2
Ingredients:
- 1 big cucumber, peeled and chopped
- 1 zucchini, peeled and chopped (steamed or lightly cooked is preferred)
- 1 cup romaine lettuce, washed
- 2 tablespoons olive oil
- Himalaya salt to taste

Instructions:

1. Place all the ingredients in a blender.
2. Process well until smooth.
3. Serve and enjoy!

Easy Tasty Sexy Red Smoothie

Red bell peppers taste great in smoothies.
They are naturally sweet and full of vitamins and minerals. This smoothie is especially recommended if your goal is to have healthy-looking skin.

Servings: 2
Ingredients:

- 2 red bell peppers, chopped
- 1 inch of ginger, peeled
- 2 tablespoons coconut oil
- 1 cup of coconut milk
- 1 teaspoon cinnamon powder
- Fresh ice cubes

Instructions:

1. Place all the ingredients in a blender.
2. Process well until smooth.
3. Serve and enjoy!

Creamy Choco Treat Smoothie

This smoothie recipe is amazing if you are craving something sweet and simply can't resist chocolate. Hazelnuts are one of the best nuts to use on the keto diet (they are low in carbs and full of good fats).

At the same time, stevia is a natural sweetener, and cocoa powder is a much healthier option than processed chocolate desserts.

The cinnamon powder adds I natural sweetness as well as a ton of anti-inflammatory and alkalizing properties. Even if your goal is to lose weight, you can still enjoy this guilt-free smoothie as a yummy, healthy dessert!

Servings: 2

Ingredients:

- 1 big avocado
- 1 tablespoon cinnamon powder
- 1 cup full fat coconut milk or coconut cream
- 1 tablespoon coconut oil
- 3 tablespoons raw cocoa powder
- 1 tablespoon Organifi green powder (optional)
- 1 tablespoon chia seeds or chia seed powder
- A handful of hazelnuts crashed
- Stevia to sweeten (optional)

Instructions:

1. Process all the ingredients (except hazelnuts) in a blender until super smooth.
2. Serve in dessert bowls, preferably chilled.

3. Add in the hazelnuts and sweeten with stevia if needed.
4. You can also add in 1 teaspoon of Organifi green powder. It's totally optional but makes smoothies taste really lovely and naturally sweet and adds in a ton of superfoods.

You can learn more about it on my website:

www.YourWellnessBooks.com/resources

Refreshing Herbal Weight Loss Smoothie

This is a straightforward and all-natural smoothie recipe that uses fennel tea as well as grapefruits- both ingredients are super alkaline as well as keto friendly and fantastic for natural weight loss. They are low in carbs and high in nutrients.

This smoothie can be made both in the summer as well as in the winter version...

Summer Version – to Chill Out

Servings: 2

Ingredients:

- 1 cup fennel tea, chilled (use 2 fennel tea bags per 1 cup of water)
- 1 grapefruit, peeled
- Half cup ice cubes
- 2 tablespoons coconut oil
- Stevia to sweeten if needed
- A few mint leaves to garnish

Instructions:

1. Place all the ingredients in a blender.
2. Process until smooth.
3. Sweeten with stevia if needed.
4. Serve in a tall smoothie glass, or glasses, garnish with fresh mint leaves, serve and enjoy!

Winter Version- Cosy & Comforting

Servings: 2

Ingredients:

- 1 cup fennel tea, warm, but not too hot (use 2 fennel tea bags per 1 cup of water)
- 1 grapefruit, peeled
- 1 cup full fat coconut milk, warm, but not too hot
- 2 tablespoons coconut oil
- Stevia to sweeten if needed
- A few mint leaves to garnish

Instructions:

1. Place all the ingredients in a blender.
2. Process until smooth.
3. Sweeten with stevia if needed.
4. Serve in a smoothie glass, garnish with fresh mint leaves, serve and enjoy!

Creamy a la Mojito Smoothie

This recipe is a non-alcoholic, super refreshing alkaline keto smoothie version of a mojito. Perfect for hot summer days!

Servings: 2

Ingredients:

- 2 limes, peeled and sliced
- 1 cup crushed ice
- 2 tablespoons coconut oil
- A handful of fresh mint
- Stevia to sweeten
- A pinch of Himalaya salt

Instructions:

1. Blend all the ingredients in a blender
2. Serve cold and enjoy!

Iron Rich Smoothie for Optimal Energy

This smoothie is very beginner friendly and contains the best of the alkaline keto worlds. Spinach blends really well with limes. Vitamin C helps in Iron absorption, and this smoothie is perfect if you need more energy.

Servings:2

Ingredients:

- 1 cup baby spinach leaves
- 2 limes, peeled and sliced
- 1 cup thick coconut milk
- 2 tablespoons coconut oil
- Pinch of nutmeg and cinnamon
- Optional: stevia or Organifi powder to sweeten

Instructions:

1. Combine all the ingredients in a blender.
2. Process well until smooth.
3. Serve and enjoy!

Forest Fruit Creamy Smoothie

This is one of my favorite creamy smoothie recipes. It's perfect as a quick, guilt-free dessert too and can be easily turned into an alkaline keto friendly smoothie bowl (just add in some nuts and seeds).

Servings: 2

Ingredients:

- 1 cup full-fat Greek Yoghurt (unsweetened)
- 1 tablespoon coconut oil
- 10 organic strawberries
- 1 teaspoon maca powder
- Stevia or organific powder to sweeten

What I love about Organifi powder, is that it allows me to get my daily portion of greens and other superfoods. It works very well when I am too busy to go shopping, wash the greens, etc.

And again, it tastes really lovely with Greek yogurt and makes this recipe more alkaline too!

You can learn more about it and other helpful resources and supplements that I use at:

www.YourWellnessBooks.com/resources

Morning on the Go Chia Smoothie

Chia seeds are jam-packed with vital nutrients. They are a fantastic source of omega-3 fatty acids, full of antioxidants, and they also provide fiber, iron, and calcium.

Servings: 1-2

Ingredients:

- 1 small green apple, seeds removed
- A handful of spinach, or other greens of your choice
- 1 cup coconut milk or Greek Yoghurt
- 2 tablespoons chia seeds
- 2 tablespoons coconut oil
- 1 teaspoon cinnamon powder

Instructions:

1. Place all the ingredients in a blender.
2. Process well until smooth.
3. Serve and enjoy!

Spicy Broccoli Smoothie

I love this smoothie on my detox days. While, my regular diet is a balanced, clean food diet with a ton of keto and alkaline friendly foods (and some mini cheats occasionally), once or twice a year I like to go on a little detox- a food cleanse where I eat only alkaline foods. Actually, I love it so much that now I do it twice a year. It's an excellent self-development experience, you get to release the toxins and old patterns to embrace the new energies and opportunities. Not to mention the weight loss and healthy glow!

If you would like to learn more about the cleanse I like to do, I highly recommend Yuri Elkaim's program. You can learn more about it on my website:

www.YourWellnessBooks.com/resources

Perhaps you feel like the constant sugar cravings you are getting are sabotaging your health and weight loss goals. I have been there. Luckily, after going through the program, everything has changed for me (in a positive way).

Now...back to our detox smoothie. Like most vegetable smoothies, it can also be turned into a delicious soup.

Servings: 2

Ingredients:

- 1 cup broccoli florets, steamed or lightly cooked
- 1 garlic clove, peeled
- 1 chili flake or a pinch of chili powder
- A pinch of nutmeg powder
- A pinch of curry powder
- 1 cup full fat coconut milk

- 2 tablespoons coconut oil, or flax seed oil
- A handful of chive, minced

Instructions:

1. Place all the ingredients except chive in a blender.
2. Process well until smooth.
3. If needed, warm it up and serve as a soup, with some fresh chive in it.
4. Enjoy!

Questions?

You can email me at:

info@yourwellnessbooks.com

Alkaline Ketogenic Smoothies is the second book in the Alkaline Keto Diet Book series.

The first book in the series is called: *Alkaline Ketogenic Mix*: *Quick, Easy, and Delicious Recipes & Tips for Natural Weight Loss and a Healthy Lifestyle.*
It's a step-by-step beginner guide to help you transition to a healthy alkaline-keto way of eating without feeling deprived.

You will find all the Alkaline Keto Diet books on Amazon & listed on our website:

www.amazon.com/author/elenagarcia

www.yourwellnessbooks.com/books

Extra Resources to Help You on Your Journey

I am regularly updating my website with new health and wellness recommendations (books, resources, natural supplements, and products).

My purpose and mission is to help you with easy-to-follow guides while sharing what has worked for me on my journey.

The goal is to keep it very simple, doable, and fun to help you enjoy vibrant health and, if desired, start losing weight (naturally).

Wellness doesn't have to be complicated or expensive. Quite on the contrary.

What matters is the actions you decide to take right here, right now. Little, imperfect but meaningful actions will lead you to beautiful results as the compound effect will start taking place.

Thank you again for reading.

I am really grateful for you,

Until next time,

Wishing you all the best on your journey,

Elena

We Need Your Help

One more thing, before you go, could you please do us a quick favor?

It would be great if you could leave us a short review online.

Don't worry, it doesn't have to be long. One sentence is enough.

Let others know your favorite recipes and who you think this book can help.

Many people drink "normal" smoothies and don't even realize they are overdoing sugar and carbs. No wonder they give up...

Your review can inspire more and more people to turn to low-carb, low-sugar nutrient-packed smoothies so that they can finally achieve their wellness and weight loss goals the way they deserve.

Your honest review is critical.

Thank You for your support!

Join Our VIP Readers' Newsletter to Boost Your Wellbeing

Would you like to be notified about our new health and wellness books?

How about receiving them at deeply discounted prices? And before anyone else?

What about awesome giveaways, latest health tips, and motivation?

If that is something you are interested in, please visit the link below to join our newsletter:

www.yourwellnessbooks.com/email-newsletter

It's 100% free + spam free (we hate spam as much as you do)

We promise we will only email you with valuable and relevant information, delicious recipes, and tips to help you on your journey.

Sign up link:

www.yourwellnessbooks.com/email-newsletter

More Books & Resources in the Healthy Lifestyle Series

Available at:

www.yourwellnessbooks.com

A physician has not written the information in this book. It is advisable that you visit a qualified dietician so that you can obtain a highly personalized treatment for your case, especially if you want to lose weight effectively. This book is for informational and educational purposes only and is not intended for medical purposes. Please consult your physician before making any drastic changes to your diet.

All information in this book has been carefully researched and checked for factual accuracy. However, the author and publishers make no warranty, expressed or implied, that the information contained herein is appropriate for every individual, situation or purpose, and assume no responsibility for errors or omission. The reader assumes the risk, and full responsibility for all actions and the author will not be held liable for any loss or damage, whether consequential, incidental, and special or otherwise, that may result from the information presented in this publication.

The book is not intended to provide medical advice or to take the place of medical advice and treatment from your personal physician. Readers are advised to consult their own doctors or other qualified health professionals regarding the treatment of medical conditions. The author shall not be held liable or responsible for any misunderstanding or misuse of the information contained in this book. The information is not intended to diagnose, treat, or cure any disease.

If you suffer from any medical condition, are pregnant, lactating, or on medication, be sure to talk to your doctor before making any drastic changes in your diet and lifestyle.

CPSIA information can be obtained
at www.ICGtesting.com
Printed in the USA
LVHW021159280720
661663LV00020B/466